a ghost story for theatre
CARMILLA

BY ADAM YEE
AFTER THE NOVELLA BY
SHERIDAN LE FANU

Currency Press,
Sydney

LA MAMA

CURRENT THEATRE SERIES

First published in 2018
by Currency Press Pty Ltd,
PO Box 2287, Strawberry Hills, NSW, 2012, Australia
enquiries@currency.com.au
www.currency.com.au

in association with La Mama Theatre, Melbourne

Typeset by Dean Nottle for Currency Press.
Cover design by Emma Bennetts for Currency Press.
Front cover shows Jacques-Emile Blanche's The pink rose 1890, oil on canvas;
65.4 x 81.6, National Gallery of Victoria, Melbourne.
The full musical score is available for download at: https://wordpress.com/view/
carmillatheopera.wordpress.com

NATIONAL
LIBRARY
OF AUSTRALIA

A catalogue record for this
book is available from the
National Library of Australia

Contents

Currency Press acknowledges the Traditional Owners of the Country on which we live and work. We pay our respects to all Aboriginal and Torres Strait Islander Elders, past and present.

Carmilla

N.B. hereafter, double bar lines indicate a silent pause, responsive to the stage action.

Very Slow ♩<40

Flute — *ppp*

Tenor Saxophone — *ppp*

Violin — con sord. *ppp*

Violoncello — con sord. *ppp*

Harmonium RH — *ppp*

Piano — *ppp*

In the raptures of my enormous humiliation I live in your warm life ... O you shall die sweetly die into mine ... I cannot help it as I draw near to you

you in your turn will draw near to others ... & learn the rapture of that cruelty, which yet is love

NOTES ON THE PRODUCTION

Set in the late eighteenth century, *Carmilla* is opera in its etymological sense; it is a 'working through' of music and drama. More strictly, though, it is a melodrama, a spoken text interwoven with almost continuous musical commentary.

This is not a radio play, however. The staging is vital to the storytelling. Locations and staging directions (most of which are paraphrased from the novella) are intended as suggestions only. *Carmilla* could be performed in near darkness, illuminated by candles and lamps. *Carmilla* could also be staged in miniature, using dolls, small handmade objects, dolls houses et cetera.

The opening chorale presents the entire harmonic argument of the opera. The thematic material is derived from Carmilla's speech: 'In the rapture of my enormous humiliation ...' and is developed anagrammatically, just as her name is transformed in the novella (e.g. Mircalla, Millarca).

Much of the score relates to the proportion set 1:2:4:7.

Adam Yee, Composer / Librettist

Carmilla was first produced at La Mama Courthouse Theatre, Melbourne, on 15 December 2016, as part of La Mama's Explorations Season, with the following cast:

LAURA	Georgia Brooks
CARMILLA	Anna Burley
LAURA'S FATHER	Joshua Porter
GENERAL SPIELSDORF	Amit Golder
BERTHA / PEASANT GIRL	Danielle Carey
MUSICIANS	Elizabeth Barcan (flute),
	Pri Victor (tenor saxophone)
	Lyndon Chester (violin)
	Rosanne Hunt (cello)
	Eidit Golder (piano)
	Matan Franco (harmonium right hand and quartertone glockenspiel)

Conductor, Tom Pugh
Director, Karen Wakeham
Designer, Helen Rofe
Lighting Designer, Emma Fox
Stage Manager, Melanie Belcher

CHARACTERS

LAURA

CARMILLA

LAURA'S FATHER

GENERAL SPIELSDORF

YOUNG LAURA / PEASANT GIRL / BERTHA (non-speaking)

The voice of LAURA'S MOTHER can be spoken by an orchestra member or the actor who plays BERTHA.

Several other non-speaking roles may be taken by the instrumentalists:

Flute
Tenor Saxophone
Violin
Cello
Harmonium/Organ (right hand) doubling Quartertone Glockenspiel
Piano

SETTING

Late eighteenth century, Styria.

NOTE

Throughout the libretto, words in **bold** text cue the music they precede.

This play went to press before the end of rehearsals and may differ from the play as performed.

A spotlight comes up on LAURA.

LAURA: In Styria, we, though by no means magnificent people, inhabit a castle, or *schloss*.

Nothing can be more picturesque or **solitary**.

I must tell you of the first occurrence in my existence, which produced a terrible impression upon my mind. It was one of the very earliest incidents of my life which I can recollect. I was not frightened, for I was one of those happy children who are studiously kept in ignorance of **ghost** stories.

> *Lights reveal* YOUNG LAURA, *asleep in her bed.*
>
> *She wakes, and realises that she is alone.*
>
> CARMILLA *appears, looking at* YOUNG LAURA.
>
> CARMILLA *caresses* YOUNG LAURA, *lies down beside her on the bed, and draws* YOUNG LAURA *towards her, smiling.*
>
> YOUNG LAURA *is soothed and sleeps.*
>
> *Suddenly,* CARMILLA *leans over* YOUNG LAURA *who wakes, startled, and cries out loudly.*
>
> CARMILLA *starts back, with her eyes fixed on* YOUNG LAURA, *and then vanishes.*
>
> *The lights on the bed fade out.*

LAURA'S FATHER: Do not be frightened. It was nothing but a dream. It cannot hurt you.

LAURA: But I was not comforted, for I knew the visit of the strange woman had been real.

> *Blackout.*

▼ ▼ ▼ ▼ ▼

LAURA: I am now going to tell you something so strange that it will require all your faith in my veracity to believe my **story**.

> *Lights reveal* LAURA *and her* FATHER *as they enter together.* LAURA'S FATHER *is reading a letter.*

LAURA'S FATHER: General Spielsdorf cannot come to us so soon as I had hoped.

LAURA: And how soon does he come?

LAURA'S FATHER: Not for two months, I dare say. And I am very glad now, dear, that you never knew Mademoiselle Rheinfeldt.

LAURA: And why?

LAURA'S FATHER: Because the poor young lady is **dead**.

> *He hands the letter to* LAURA.

His letter appears to me to have been written very nearly in distraction.

LAURA: [*reading*] 'I have **lost** my darling daughter, for as such I loved her.

'I had no idea of her danger. I have lost her, and now learn all too late. She died in the peace of innocence. The fiend who betrayed our infatuated hospitality has done it all. I thought I was receiving into my house innocence, gaiety, a charming companion for my lost Bertha. Heavens!

'What a **fool** I have been! I devote my remaining days to tracking and extinguishing a monster, cursing my conceited incredulity, my despicable affectation of superiority, my blindness, my obstinacy—all too late. I cannot write or talk collectedly now.

'Farewell. Pray for me, dear **friend**.'

> LAURA*'s eyes fill with tears.*
> *The sun sets.*
> LAURA *hands the letter back to her* FATHER.

LAURA'S FATHER: I feel as if some great misfortune were **hanging** over us.

> *There is a sound of carriage wheels and hoofs upon the road.*
>
> LAURA *is afraid, but runs towards the carriage.*
>
> *She leans over the unconscious body of* CARMILLA, *who has been thrown clear.*
>
> CARMILLA'*s face is completely masked by long, dark hair.*
>
> LAURA'S FATHER *approaches, and takes* CARMILLA'*s pulse.*
>
> *Together, they lift* CARMILLA *and exit.*
>
> **Blackout.**

▼ ▼ ▼ ▼ ▼

LAURA *is in a **spotlight**,* CARMILLA *in bed.*

LAURA: [*delighted*] You, who live in towns, can have no idea how great an event the introduction of a new friend can be, in such a solitude as surrounded **us**.

> LAURA *approaches* CARMILLA.
>
> CARMILLA *brushes her hair aside, revealing her face.*
>
> LAURA *starts back in recognition.*
>
> CARMILLA'*s melancholy expression instantly lights into a strange, fixed smile of recognition.*

CARMILLA: How wonderful! Twelve years ago, I saw your face in a dream, and it has haunted me ever **since**.

LAURA: Wonderful indeed!

[*Suppressing horror*] Twelve years ago, in vision or reality, I certainly saw you. I could not forget your face. It has remained before my eyes ever **since**.

> CARMILLA'*s smile softens.*
>
> LAURA *sits on the bed, and takes* CARMILLA'*s hand.*

CARMILLA lays her hand upon LAURA*'s, and her eyes glow. She looks hastily into* LAURA*'s eyes, smiles again, and blushes.*

LAURA *returns her smile in wonderment.*

CARMILLA: I have never had a friend—shall I find one **now**?

CARMILLA sighs, gazing passionately at LAURA.

LAURA *is both drawn to* CARMILLA *and somewhat repulsed.*

Languor and exhaustion steal over CARMILLA.

She holds LAURA *close for a minute and whispers in her ear.*

Goodnight, darling, it is very hard to part with you, but goodnight; tomorrow, but not early, I shall see you **again**.

CARMILLA sinks back on the pillow with a sigh, her eyes following LAURA *with a fond and melancholy gaze.*

Goodnight, dear friend.

LAURA *exits.*

Blackout.

▼ ▼ ▼ ▼ ▼

A spotlight on LAURA.

LAURA: I was **charmed** with Carmilla, but there was a coldness, it seemed to me, beyond her years. She would not tell me the name of her family, nor even that of the country they lived in.

She used to place her pretty arms about my neck, draw me to her, and laying her cheek to mine, murmur with her lips near my ear:

CARMILLA: [*emerging from the darkness*] **Dearest**, your little heart is wounded; if your dear heart is wounded, my wild heart bleeds with yours.

Very slow, coordinated with piano cues:

LAURA: She used to place her pretty arms about my neck, draw me to her, and laying her cheek to mine, murmur with her lips near my ear:
CARMILLA: [Emerging from the darkness:] **Dearest**, your little heart is wounded; if your dear heart is wounded, my wild heart bleeds with yours.

CARMILLA: [Very slow, co-ordinated with piano cues.] In the rapture of my enormous humiliation, I live in your warm life. And you shall die, sweetly die, Into mine.

CARMILLA: I cannot help it. As I draw near to you, You in your turn Will draw near to others.

CARMILLA: And learn the rapture of that cruelty Which yet is love. So for a while, seek to know no more of me and mine, [even slower] But trust me with all your loving spirit. [CARMILLA returns to the darkness.]

In the rapture of my enormous humiliation I live in your warm life, and you shall die—die, sweetly die—into mine. I cannot help it; as I draw near to you, you, in your turn, will draw near to others, and learn the rapture of that cruelty, which yet is love; so, for a while, seek to know no more of me and mine, but trust me with all your loving spirit.

    CARMILLA *returns to the darkness.*

LAURA: **And** when she had spoken such a rhapsody, she would press me more closely in her trembling embrace.

I used to wish to extricate myself; but my energies seemed to fail me. Her murmured words sounded like a lullaby in my ear, and soothed my resistance into a trance.

Hers was like the ardor of a lover. It embarrassed me; it was hateful and yet overpowering. And with gloating eyes she drew me to her, and her hot lips travelled along my cheek in kisses; and she would whisper, almost in sobs:

CARMILLA: [*again emerging from the darkness*] You are mine, you shall be mine, you and I are one for ever.

LAURA: [*to* CARMILLA, *angrily*] **What** can you mean by all this? I hate it. I don't know you—I don't know myself when you look so and talk so.

    CARMILLA *sighs, turns away, and drops* LAURA's *hand.*

    Blackout.

▼ ▼ ▼ ▼ ▼

*A **funeral procession** passes by* LAURA *and* CARMILLA.

Mourners are humming a funeral hymn (the top notes of the piano chords).

LAURA, *out of respect, joins in the humming.*

CARMILLA *shakes her arm, a little roughly.*

Slightly slower and very free in time

CARMILLA'S line is cued by the G major choral

CARMILLA: [Again emerging from darkness:]
You are mine, you shall be mine, you and I are one forever.

LAURA: [To CARMILLA, angrily:] What can you mean by all this? I hate it. I don't know you — I don't know myself when you look so and talk so.

molto rall.

accel.

rall.

[CARMILLA sighs, turns away, and drops LAURA'S hand. Blackout.]

CARMILLA: Don't you perceive how discordant that is?

LAURA: I think it very sweet, on the contrary.

*LAURA resumes her **humming**.*

CARMILLA: [*almost angrily*] You pierce my ears!

She stops her ears with her fingers.

I hate funerals. What a fuss! Why, you must die—everyone must die; and all are happier when they do.

LAURA: She is the poor girl who fancied she saw a ghost a fortnight **ago**.

CARMILLA: Tell me nothing about ghosts. I shan't sleep tonight if you do.

LAURA: I hope there is no plague or fever coming. The swineherd's young wife died only a week ago. She thought something seized her by the throat as she lay in her bed, and nearly **strangled** her.

They resume their seat on the bench.

CARMILLA: Are you afraid, dearest?

LAURA: I should be very much. If I fancied there was any real danger of my being attacked as those poor people **were**.

CARMILLA: You are afraid to die?

LAURA: Yes, everyone is.

CARMILLA: But to die as lovers may—to die together, so that they may live together?

Blackout.

▼ ▼ ▼ ▼ ▼

*LAURA is **taking** an old portrait from a picture box.*

LAURA: Carmilla, dear, here is an absolute miracle. Here you are, living, smiling, ready to speak, in this picture. Isn't it beautiful, Papa? And see, even the little mole on her throat.

LAURA'S FATHER: [*laughing*] Certainly it is a wonderful **likeness**.

LAURA: Will you let me hang this picture in my room, Papa?

LAURA'S FATHER: Certainly, dear. I'm very glad you think it so like. It must be prettier even than I thought it, if it is.

LAURA: You can read quite plainly the name that is written in the corner. Mircalla, Countess Karnstein, and this is a little coronet over and underneath A.D. 1698. I am descended from the Karnsteins; that is, Mama **was**.

CARMILLA: [*languidly*] Ah! so am I, I think, a very long descent, very ancient. Are there any Karnsteins living now?

LAURA: The family was ruined, I believe, in some civil wars, long ago, but the stones of the castle are only about three miles **away**.

CARMILLA: How interesting! But see what beautiful moonlight. Suppose you take a little ramble round the garden with me, and look down at the road and river.

LAURA: It is so like the night you came to **us**.

> CARMILLA *sighs, smiling.*
>
> *She and* LAURA *twine their arms about each other's waists as they walk outside, slowly, in silence.*

CARMILLA: [*almost whispering*] And so you were thinking of the night I came here? Are you glad I came?

LAURA: Delighted, dear Carmilla. How romantic you are.

> CARMILLA **kisses** LAURA *silently.*

I am sure that you have been in love. That there is, at this moment, an affair of the heart going on.

CARMILLA: I have been in love with no-one, and never shall. [*Whispering*] Unless it should be with you.

> CARMILLA *quickly hides her face in* LAURA's *neck and hair, with tumultuous sighs, that seem almost to sob, and presses a trembling hand into* LAURA's.

CARMILLA *puts her cheek to* LAURA*'s.*

Darling, darling. I live in you; and you would die for me, I love you so.

LAURA *starts from her.*

LAURA: You look ill, Carmilla; a little faint. You certainly must take some wine.

CARMILLA: Let us look again for a moment; it is the last time, perhaps, I shall see the moonlight with you.

LAURA: [*alarmed*] How do you feel now, dear Carmilla? Are you really better? We have a very skilful doctor near us, the physician who was with Papa today.

CARMILLA: I'm sure he is. I know how kind you all are; but, dear child, I am quite well again. There is nothing ever wrong with me, but a little weakness.

Blackout.

▼ ▼ ▼ ▼ ▼

LAURA *and* CARMILLA **prepare** *for bed.*

CARMILLA: The time is very near when you shall know everything. You will think me cruel, very selfish, yet you must come with me, loving me, to death; or else hate me, and still come with me, and hating me through death and after.

LAURA: [*nervously*] Now, Carmilla, you are going to talk your wild nonsense **again**.

CARMILLA: I see it all, as divers see what is going on above them, through a medium: dense, rippling, but transparent. It's as it was the night after a long-ago ball. I was all but assassinated in my bed, wounded here [*touching her breast*] and never was the same since.

LAURA: Were you near dying?

CARMILLA: Yes, very—a cruel love—strange love, that would have taken my **life**.

Love will have its sacrifices. No sacrifice is without blood. Let us go to sleep now; I feel so lazy. How can I possibly get up just now and lock my door?

LAURA: Goodnight.

> LAURA *enters her room.*
>
> *She sleeps and begins to* ***dream***.
>
> *A sooty black animal, resembling a monstrous cat, is moving around the foot of the bed.*
>
> LAURA *watches in terror, unable to cry out.*
>
> *The shape* ***springs*** *onto the bed, and* LAURA *feels a stinging pain as if two large needles darted, an inch or two apart, deep into her breast.*
>
> *Blackout.*

▼ ▼ ▼ ▼ ▼

LAURA *wakes with a* ***scream***.

She sees a female figure standing at the foot of the bed.

The figure is in a dark, loose dress, its hair is down, covering its shoulders.

The figure is completely still, and is not breathing.

Blackout.

▼ ▼ ▼ ▼ ▼

LAURA: Carmilla became more devoted to me than ever. She used to gloat with an ardor that grew stronger as my strength and spirits waned. This always **shocked** me. It was like a momentary glare of insanity.

For without knowing it, I was suffering the strangest **illness**.

Certain vague sensations visited me in my sleep. There were **dreams** that seemed interminable, but I could never recollect their scenery or any persons that inhabited them. But they left an awful impression, and a sense of exhaustion, as if I had passed through a long period of great mental exertion and danger.

Sometimes there came another sensation as if a hand was drawing itself softly along my cheek and neck. Sometimes warm lips **kissed** me, longer and longer and more and more lovingly, until they reached my throat. My heart beat faster. My breathing rose and fell rapidly.

A sobbing, that rose into a sense of strangulation, supervened, and turned into a dreadful convulsion, until at last my senses left me. Finally I became **unconscious**.

> LAURA *returns to her sick bed.*

LAURA'S MOTHER: [*a voice, screaming*] Your mother warns you to beware of the assassin!

> *Immediately we see* CARMILLA, *standing, near the foot of the bed, in a white nightdress, bathed, from her chin to her feet, in one great stain of blood.*
>
> LAURA *wakens with a* **shriek**, *springs from her bed, screaming and crying for help.*
>
> *She desperately knocks on* CARMILLA'*s locked door.*
>
> LAURA'S FATHER *enters and forces the door.*
>
> *They search the empty room thoroughly.*

LAURA: Papa! Carmilla has disappeared!

LAURA'S FATHER: We must find her.

> *They* **search** *the* schloss *thoroughly.*
>
> *Finally,* LAURA *runs back into* CARMILLA'*s room and* **finds** *her.*
>
> LAURA *is astounded.*

LAURA: Sometimes there came another sensation as if a hand was drawing itself softly along my cheek and neck. Sometimes warm lips **kissed me,** longer and longer and more and more lovingly until they reached my throat. My heart beat faster. My breathing rose and fell rapidly. A sobbing, that rose into a sense of strangulation, supervened, and turned into a dreadful convulsion, until at last my senses left me. Finally I became unconscious. [LAURA returns to her sick bed.]

> CARMILLA *beckons silently to* LAURA.
>
> CARMILLA'*s face expresses extreme fear.*
>
> LAURA *runs to her in an ecstasy of joy.*
>
> LAURA *kisses her and embraces* CARMILLA *again and again.*

LAURA: **Dear** Carmilla, what has become of you all this time? We have been in agonies of anxiety. Where have you been? How did you come back?

CARMILLA: Last night has been a night of wonders.

> *Pause.*

It was past two o'clock when I went to sleep as usual in my bed, with my doors locked. I woke just now on the sofa in the dressing room there, and I found both doors **open**. One had been forced. How could all this have happened without my being wakened?

> LAURA'S FATHER *enters.*
>
> *He takes a turn up and down the room, thinking.*
>
> CARMILLA'*s eye follows him for a moment with a sly, dark glance.*
>
> LAURA'S FATHER *comes to* CARMILLA *thoughtfully, takes her hand very kindly.*

My **story** is simply one of bewilderment and darkness. I know absolutely nothing.

LAURA'S FATHER: Have you ever been suspected of walking in your sleep?

CARMILLA: Yes; I know I did. I have been told so often by my old nurse.

> LAURA'S FATHER *smiles and nods.*

LAURA: And how, Papa, do you account for her finding herself on the sofa in the dressing room? We searched so carefully.

LAURA'S FATHER: She came there after you had searched it, still in her sleep, and at last awoke spontaneously. I think she was as much surprised to find herself where she was as anyone else. [*Laughing*] I wish all mysteries were as easily and innocently explained as yours, Carmilla.

> LAURA'S FATHER *regards* CARMILLA, *who looks charmingly well.*

[*Aside, sighing*] I wish my poor Laura was looking more like **herself**.

Blackout.

▼ ▼ ▼ ▼ ▼

A DOCTOR **examines** LAURA, *listens to her heartbeat, and is looking increasingly grave. There is a dash of horror in his expression.*

The DOCTOR *beckons to* LAURA'S FATHER, *whose smile fades.*

They talk together, out of LAURA*'s hearing.*

LAURA'S FATHER *then holds out his hand to* LAURA; *and she here opens her collar.*

They discover the puncture wounds on her neck.

LAURA'S FATHER: [*growing pale*] God bless me!

> *The* DOCTOR **nods** *in gloomy triumph.*
>
> *He exits.*

LAURA: [*frightened*] What is it? Is there any danger?

LAURA'S FATHER: No, dear; the doctor thinks, if right steps are taken, you will be quite well again.

What you need is some fresh air. Let us go to **Karnstein**. Carmilla can follow when she comes down.

> *Blackout.*

During this blackout the orchestra lights remain on.

▼ ▼ ▼ ▼ ▼

GENERAL SPIELSDORF *enters.*

GENERAL SPIELSDORF: I should tell you all I know with pleasure but you would not believe me.

LAURA'S FATHER: Why should I not?

GENERAL SPIELSDORF: [*testily*] Because you believe in **nothing** but what consists with your own prejudices and illusions. I well remember when I was like you. But I have learned better.

LAURA'S FATHER: Try me. I am not such a dogmatist as you suppose.

GENERAL SPIELSDORF: You must understand; I have been made the dupe of a preternatural conspiracy.

> LAURA'S FATHER **glances** at GENERAL SPIELSDORF *with a marked suspicion of his sanity.*
>
> *The* GENERAL *does not see it.*

You are going to the Ruins of **Karnstein**?

LAURA'S FATHER: [*gaily*] Indeed we are. I do hope that you are thinking of claiming the title and estates for yourself?

GENERAL SPIELSDORF: [*seriously*] Something very, very different. I have strange things to tell you, my dear friend.

LAURA'S FATHER: Concerning the house of Karnstein? It has been long extinct: a hundred years at least.

GENERAL SPIELSDORF: Quite true. You saw my dear ward—my child, I may call her. No creature could have been more beautiful, and only three months ago none more blooming.

LAURA'S FATHER: Yes, poor thing! I was grieved and shocked more than I can tell you, my dear friend.

> LAURA'S FATHER **takes** *the* GENERAL*'s hand.*

Tears gather in his eyes which he does not seek to conceal.

GENERAL SPIELSDORF: [*anxiously*] How far is it to the ruins?

LAURA'S FATHER: About half a league. Pray let us hear the story you were so good as to **promise**.

> **Blackout.**
>
> *During this blackout, all orchestra members and cast put on masks.*

▼ ▼ ▼ ▼ ▼

GENERAL SPIELSDORF: The night from which my sorrow dates was devoted to a magnificent **masquerade**.

The grounds were thrown open, the trees hung with coloured lamps. There was such a display of fireworks as Paris itself had never witnessed. And such music—music, you know, is my weakness—such ravishing **music**!

The finest instrumental band, perhaps, in the world, and the finest singers who could be collected from all the great operas in Europe. As you wandered through these fantastically illuminated grounds—the moonlighted chateau throwing a rosy light from its long rows of windows—you would suddenly hear these ravishing voices stealing from the silence of some grove, or rising from boats upon the **lake**.

> BERTHA **enters** *the ballroom. She is beautiful, and is the only guest who wears no mask.*
>
> *The masked* CARMILLA *observes her with interest.*

There a beautiful young lady, with the odd name of Millarca, began a conversation with my ward.

> CARMILLA **converses** *with* BERTHA.
>
> BERTHA *admires* CARMILLA*'s dress.*

She is witty and lively and amuses CARMILLA *with laughing criticisms upon the people in the ballroom.*

After some time CARMILLA *lowers her mask.*

She amused us with lively descriptions and stories of most of the great people whom we saw upon the terrace. I liked her more and more every minute. Her gossip, without being ill-natured, was extremely diverting. I thought what life she would give to our sometimes lonely evenings at home.

CARMILLA *leaves the ball with* GENERAL SPIELSDORF *and* BERTHA.

However, Millarca complained of extreme **languor**. She was repeatedly seen in the first faint grey of the morning, crossing our park, looking like a person in a trance. This convinced me that she walked in her sleep. But how did she pass out from her room, leaving the door locked on the inside?

My dear child began to lose her looks and health, and that in a manner so mysterious, and even horrible, that I became thoroughly frightened.

She was visited by appalling **dreams**.

A vision of CARMILLA *stalking and attacking* BERTHA *in her bed.*

Then came sensations. She felt something like a pair of large needles pierce her, a little below the throat, with a very sharp pain. Then came unconsciousness. The spectre Millarca was gone. But her victim was sinking fast, and before the morning dawned, she **died**.

Long pause.

[*Indicating*] That is the chapel of the Karnsteins, down there.

LAURA'S FATHER: **We** have a portrait, at home, of Mircalla, the Countess Karnstein; should you like to see it?

GENERAL SPIELSDORF: Time enough, dear friend. For I believe that I have seen the original.

LAURA'S FATHER: What?! Seen the Countess Mircalla?! Why, she has been dead more than a century!

GENERAL SPIELSDORF: Not so dead as you fancy, I am told.

There remains to me, but one object which can interest me during the few years that remain to me on earth, and that is to wreak on her the vengeance which, I thank God, may still be accomplished by a mortal arm.

LAURA'S FATHER: [*with increasing amazement*] What vengeance can you mean?

GENERAL SPIELSDORF: I mean to decapitate the **monster**.

He produces a hatchet.

LAURA'S FATHER: What?

GENERAL SPIELSDORF: To strike her head off.

LAURA'S FATHER: Cut her head off?!

Blackout.

▼ ▼ ▼ ▼ ▼

At the ruins.

LAURA **hears** CARMILLA *approach and happily goes to greet her.*

GENERAL SPIELSDORF *cries out and* **lunges** *at* CARMILLA *with the hatchet.*

A brutalised change comes over CARMILLA*'s features, instantaneous and horrible.*

GENERAL SPIELSDORF *strikes at her with all his force, but* CARMILLA *dives under the blow and catches his arm.*

He struggles, but she is in fact stronger.

The hatchet falls from his grasp and CARMILLA *flees.*

LAURA: [*starting after her*] Carmilla!

GENERAL SPIELSDORF: [*in agony*] She called herself Carmilla? Depart from this accursed ground, my poor child, as quickly as you can. Drive to the clergyman's house, and stay there till we come. Begone! May you never behold Carmilla more.

Blackout.

▼ ▼ ▼ ▼ ▼

*The Karnstein ruins, the next **day**.*

GENERAL SPIELSDORF *and* LAURA'S FATHER *consult an old manuscript to locate* CARMILLA*'s grave.*

They pull away some ivy and reveal the tomb.

The coffin is opened.

CARMILLA*'s face is tinted with life.*

They ascertain that she is breathing, and that her limbs are flexible, her flesh elastic.

Using a wooden stethoscope, they listen for, and detect, a heartbeat.

We see that the body is immersed in blood to a depth of seven inches.

The body is raised up, and a sharp stake is driven into her heart.

CARMILLA *utters a piercing shriek.*

Her head is cut off, and her body is placed on a pile of wood to be burnt.

Blackout during a pause in the music.

▼ ▼ ▼ ▼ ▼

LAURA: The following spring my father took me on a tour through **Italy**. We remained away for more than a year. It was long before the terror of recent events subsided; and to this hour the image of Carmilla returns to memory with ambiguous alternations.

Sometimes she is the playful, languid, beautiful girl. Sometimes she becomes the writhing **fiend** I saw in the ruined church.

Often from a reverie I have **started**, fancying I heard the light step of Carmilla at the drawing room door.

Blackout.

▼ ▼ ▼ ▼ ▼

CARMILLA, *in her bloodstained dress, is stepping lightly, in the darkness, among the audience members.*

THE END

69

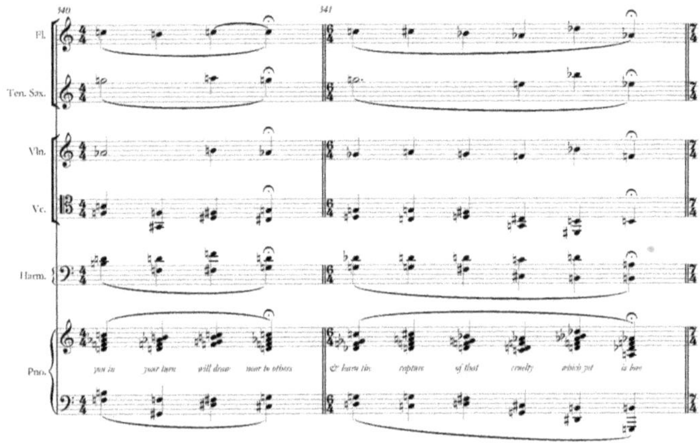

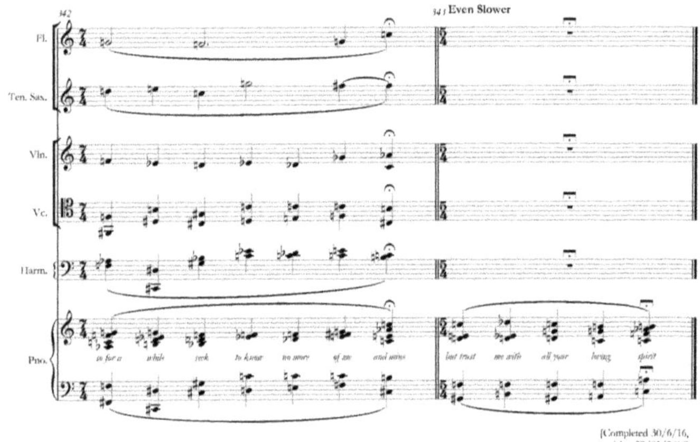

[Completed 30/6/16,
revision 28/01/2018]

LA MAMA

presents

CARMILLA

A Ghost Story for Theatre

2 May–13 May 2018

Laura
Georgia Brooks

Carmilla
Teresa Duddy

Laura's Father
Joshua Porter

General Spielsdorf
John Cheshire

Young Laura / Peasant Girl / Bertha
Danielle Carey

INSTRUMENTALISTS
Flute **Elizabeth Barcan**   Tenor Saxophone **Pri Victor**
Violin **Lyndon Chester**   Cello **Rosanne Hunt**   Piano **Eidit Golder**
Organ (right hand) / Quartertone Glockenspiel **Adam Yee**

Director
Karen Wakeman

Conductor
Tom Pugh

Lighting designer
Michael Rowe

Stage manager
Melanie Belcher

Production assistant
Hagit Pecherky

Several non-speaking roles are played by the instrumentalists.

LA MAMA

CEO & Artistic Director
Liz Jones

CEO and Manager / Producer
Caitlin Dullard

Venue Manager
Hayley Fox

Front-of-House Manager
Amber Hart

Marketing and Communications
Sophia Constantine

Design and Social Media
Jen Tran

Office Coordinator
Elena Larkin

Learning Producer and School Publications Coordinator
Maureen Hartley

Preservation Coordinator
Fiona Wiseman

La Mama Musica Curator
Annabel Warmington

La Mama Poetica Curator
Amanda Anastasi

Script Appraiser
Graham Downey

Casting Service
Zac Kazepis

Level 1, 205 Faraday Street, Carlton VIC 3053
www.lamama.com.au | info@lamama.com.au
facebook.com/lamama.theatre | twitter.com/lamamatheatre
Office phone 03 9347 6948 | Office Mon–Fri, 10:30am–5:30pm

FRONT OF HOUSE STAFF

Susan Bamford-Caleo, Carmelina Di Guglielmo, Laurence Strangio, Dennis Coard, Darren Vizer, Robyn Clancy, Zac Kazepis, Aaron Bradbrook, Anna Ellis, Alex Woollatt, Annie Thorald, Helen Doig.

COMMITTEE OF MANAGEMENT

Sue Broadway, David Levin, Caroline Lee, Dur-é Dara, Richard Watts, Helen Hopkins, Beng Oh, Ben Grant, Liz Jones.

Our sincerest thanks to the many volunteers who generously give their time in support of La Mama.

La Mama's Committee of Management, staff and its wider theatrical community acknowledge that our theatre is on traditional Wurundjeri land.

The La Mama community acknowledges the considerable support it has received in the past decade from Jeanne Pratt and The Pratt Foundation.

La Mama is financially assisted by the Australian Government through the Australia Council – its arts funding and advisory body, the Victorian Government through Creative Victoria – Department of Premier and Cabinet, and the City of Melbourne through the Arts and Culture triennial funding program.

Australian Government

Australia Council
for the Arts

CREATIVE VICTORIA

CITY OF MELBOURNE

DIRECTOR'S NOTE

This production began with its music, which came from two sources: Adam's score and the music of Le Fanu's poetry.

Placing the orchestra in view is a form of non-naturalism that ensures the musicians' contribution to the visual as well as the usual auditory aspects of stagecraft, so all performers and designers can create together the shifting moods of the story. In this we catch the spirit of eighteenth century French *mélodrame*—that the intense poetries of Carmilla's darknesses may be realised.

Karen Wakeham, Director

LIGHTING DESIGNER'S NOTE

Lighting design often comes later in the creative process, when the Director's and Designer's vision has started to take shape. For me the process starts with the source material and relevant background research—in this case, early vampire literature including Dracula and Polidari's *The Vampyre*—which informs the motivation and aesthetic of the design and the demands of the space.

The gothic darkness of *Carmilla* comes from contrast and selectively revealing just enough form to create the space and mood.

Michael Rowe, Lighting Designer

THANKS TO

Our Production Assistant, Hagit Pechersky; Wendy Drowley and Heidelberg Theatre Company for costumes; Maureen Hartley, La Mama Learning Producer; Andre Branda-Pawlaczyk from Your Show for his technical advice; Liz Jones and everyone at La Mama.

J SHERIDAN LE FANU
WRITER

ADAM YEE
WRITER / MUSICIAN

J Sheridan Le Fanu (28 August 1814–7 February 1873) was an Irish writer of Gothic tales and mystery novels. He was a leading ghost story writer of the nineteenth century and was central to the development of the genre in the Victorian era. Three of his best-known works are *Uncle Silas*, *Carmilla*, and *The House By The Churchyard*.

Adam Yee is a composer, Head of Music at King David School and Melbourne University. He wrote his first opera *Don't Open the Door* at age 17 just after finishing his final VCE exam. He is a graduate of the VCA, Melbourne University and the RMIT Spatial Information Architecture Laboratory, and is currently a PhD Candidate in the Education Faculty at Monash. He has been a contributor to VCE curriculum development since 2005. *Carmilla* is his fifth stage work. Adam's previous shows at La Mama include *Don't Open the Door* (1992), *The Road to Hell is Paved With Slaughter* (1993) and *Bangers* (1994).

KAREN WAKEHAM
DIRECTOR

MELANIE BELCHER
STAGE MANAGER

Carmilla is **Karen Wakeham**'s sixth production at La Mama. She first worked here as a university student actor in a piece devised by Joe Bolza, then was invited by Betty Burstall to direct the very popular *Obsessive Behaviours in Small Spaces*. More recently she has directed for Heidelberg Theatre Company, classics such as *A Streetcar Named Desire*, *The Glass Menagerie*, *The Dresser* - and has a long history also in both community and independent theatre, as well as school plays, big musicals and Theatre Studies productions.

Melanie Belcher joined La Mama during the Explorations season for *Carmilla* in 2016. She has worked as Stage Manager for many more shows than she can now count (and sometimes also as Production Manager and maker-of-props), in both community and independent theatres. Some favourite productions include: *A Street Car Named Desire* and *Three Sisters* for Heidelberg Theatre Company, as well as *The Importance of Being Earnest* and *The Cripple of Inishmann*, and also Andrew Bovell's *When the Rain Stops Falling* for Not the Worst Productions last year (in 2017) at Metanoia Theatre.

MICHAEL ROWE
LIGHTING DESIGNER

TOM PUGH
CONDUCTOR

Michael Rowe spent much of his youth involved in school and community theatre. He went on to design lighting for amateur musicals in the 1990s, leading to opportunities to work on major commercial productions including *The Phantom of the Opera*, *The New Rocky Horror Show*, and *42nd Street*. He is once again active in the local theatre scene, lighting shows for Heidelberg Theatre Company, Tangled Web, and redfox3. Michael is looking forward to lighting *Carmilla*, his first production at La Mama.

Tom Pugh moved to Melbourne in 1995 to commence a Master of Music Performance in conducting at the Victorian College of the Arts, studying with Robert Rosen, Barry Bignell and Graeme Abbott. In this time he worked as an Assistant Conductor in the VCA Opera Studio and worked with numerous choirs and Musical societies. After graduating, Tom was Director of Music and Chapel Choir at Queen's College and completed a Graduate Diploma in Education at the University of Melbourne, going on to be appointed as Teacher of Flute and conductor at Brighton Grammar School in 2000, a position he held for 16 years. Tom is currently Director of Music at Flinders Christian College and Musical Director of the Mornington Peninsula Chorale.

ELIZABETH BARCAN
FLUTE

PRI VICTOR
TENOR SAXOPHONE

Melbourne flautist **Liz Barcan** is a graduate of the Victorian College of the Arts School of Music. Her career has included work with the Melbourne and Tasmanian Symphony Orchestras, the State Orchestra of Victoria, the Australian Pops Orchestra, Ariel New Music, Chamber Made Opera, Nachtmusique Chamber Ensemble, the Martin Mackerras Ensemble, Libra Ensemble and Wicked, the Musical. She played in the original 2016 production of *Carmilla* at La Mama Theatre.

Pri Victor (BMusPerf, M.Ed) has studied under distinguished Australian and international players such as Lachlan Davidson, Michael Lichnovsky, Kenneth Tse and Niels Bijl. With a dedication to teaching, Pri currently works at The King David School as well as her own private studio. She regularly performs in various chamber ensembles including the Harmonium Saxophone Quartet and Concinnity Duo, and with her husband in their jazz/funk band, Dianella Lane.

LYNDON CHESTER
VIOLIN

ROSANNE HUNT
CELLO

A classically trained violinist and composer, **Lyndon Chester** undertook his undergraduate studies at the Queensland Conservatorium of Music. In 2010, Lyndon received an Australian Post-Graduate Award and completed a Masters of Music in Performance at the University of Melbourne. He has toured and performed internationally with Amanda Palmer, Zoe Keating, Neil Gaiman and The Builders and The Butchers. He has recorded with Amanda Palmer, Neil Gaiman, Murder By Death, The Jane Austen Argument and Gemma Turvey. Lyndon has collaborated with theatre practitioners, performing, composing and creating soundscapes for The Danger Ensemble, Zen Zen Zo and Bakers Dozen.

Rosanne Hunt grew up in a family of seven where everyone played music. In the mornings, as a baby, she would lie quietly in her bassinet hearing her sisters practise violin and cello with mum in the next room. She started cello aged six (mum her first teacher), had a series of immensely enjoyable and formative experiences in youth orchestras (culminating in the 1984 Australian Youth Orchestra European Tour as principal cello), and, with detours into studying medicine and working on organic farms, eventually established a freelance life of playing (baroque and modern cello) and teaching (all ages and stages from primary to tertiary). She also runs the Hunt Family Memorial Fund which helps young musicians attend National Music Camp.

EIDIT GOLDER
PIANO

TERESA DUDDY
CARMILLA

Eidit Golder is a Melbourne-based solo pianist and chamber musician. She is currently Artistic Coordinator of the Melbourne Art Song Collective (MASC) who perform regularly at the Melbourne Recital Centre to critical acclaim. Between 2005 and 2010, Eidit was a member of the Freshwater Trio. Together with violinist Zoe Black and cellist Josephine Vains they played innovative programs at the Port Fairy Festival, Woodend Winter Arts Festival and Stradbroke Island Chamber Music Festival. Freshwater Trio was invited to play at the 2010 Vancouver International Music Festival where they received enthusiastic reviews. The Trio's concert series were regularly recorded and broadcast by the ABC, and commissioned a diverse array of compositional talent. Since forming the Melbourne Art Song Collective, Eidit has collaborated with some of Australia's foremost vocal interpreters including Merlyn Quaife, Sally-Anne Russell, Siobhan Stagg, Rosamund Illing and Michael Smallwood.

Teresa Duddy is a freelance performer and educator. She graduated from the University of Melbourne with a Bachelor of Music, Chicago College of Performing Arts with a Masters of Opera Performance, and is currently at Deakin University doing a Masters of Teaching. Teresa has performed in Australia and internationally in opera, musical theatre, and as an actor on stage and television. She has worked with companies including Opera Australia, GFO, Victorian Opera, Chicago Symphony Orchestra, and Chicago Lyric Opera. She has worked in commercial and independent theatre and is excited to be performing at La Mama Theatre.

GEORGIA BROOKS
LAURA

DANIELLE CAREY
YOUNG LAURA /
PEASANT GIRL / BERTHA

A graduate of the Conservatorium at the University of Melbourne, **Georgia Brooks** is a versatile singer, actor and dancer. Georgia has appeared in operas for the Arts Centre Melbourne and Victorian Opera. With the performance group the Melbourne Rhythm Project, Georgia performed as a dancer at festivals and venues across the state. Currently, Georgia performs as a jazz singer at clubs and events around Melbourne and is working on her debut album with her band the Georgia Brooks Swingtet.

At secondary school **Danielle Carey** was awarded a music scholarship, and was later nominated for a Guild Theatre Award. She went on to study a Bachelor of Music (Voice) at Melbourne Conservatorium of Music. She has furthered her training through voice competitions, amateur musicals, opera, dance lessons, acting lessons and musical theatre programs. For her performances as Philia in UMMTA's *A Funny Thing Happened on the Way to the Chorus*, she was nominated for a Union House Theatre Performance Training Scholarship.

JOSHUA PORTER
LAURA'S FATHER

Josh Porter's performance background has largely been in comedy. He is part of the duo Game Boys who have a YouTube series and have performed live at the last three Melbourne Fringe Festivals and Melbourne International Comedy Festivals. Last year they were nominated for the Golden Gibbo, an award which celebrates a local, independent act that 'bucks trends and pursues the artist's idea more strongly than it pursues any commercial lure'. Josh is also one third of comedy podcast Welcome to Patchwork.

JOHN CHESHIRE
GENERAL SPIELSDORF

A Conservatorium dropout, **John Cheshire** graduated in Performing Arts at Deakin University. John then worked professionally at Arena Theatre for three years, touring twelve plays to schools and festivals in Australia and Canada. Leaving a career in the arts for social work, John took to community theatre to keep sane. John has performed in numerous plays over the past few decades. One of his favourite roles, Norman in The Dresser, was brought to life under Karen Wakeham's direction at Heidelberg Theatre. John is grateful to have the opportunity to explore our darker imaginings with Karen in Carmilla.

STANDING OVATION FOR
AUSTRALIA'S HOME OF INDEPENDENT THEATRE

In 2018 La Mama will celebrate 51 years of nurturing new Australian theatre.

Built in 1883 for Anthony Reuben Ford, a Carlton printer, the building at 205 Faraday Street had been used as a workshop, a boot and shoe factory, an electrical engineering workshop and a silk underwear factory before becoming a theatre in 1967. La Mama was established by Betty Burstall and modelled on experimental theatre activities at La MaMa E.T.C., New York. Jack Hibberd's play *Three Old Friends* was the first play performed in the tiny space.

Since that time the crowded intimacy of La Mama has provided welcome opportunities to a host of playwrights, actors, directors, technicians, film-makers, poets and comedians, such as David Williamson, Barry Dickins, John Romeril, Tes Lyssiotis, Lloyd Jones, Arthur and Corinne Cantrill, Judith Lucy, Richard Frankland, Julia Zemiro, and Cate Blanchett... the list of those who have been nurtured there is long.

Under the capable care of Liz Jones (Artistic Director since 1976), and her La Mama team, more than 50 productions are now produced annually at La Mama, and at our second performance venue, the refurbished La Mama Courthouse, 349 Drummond Street. An ever-increasing audience is drawn not only from the Carlton and Melbourne University environs, but from far and wide across the country.

LINKS

The Wordpress site will contain ongoing material for students studying this production and contact details. A full score is also available for download.

https://wordpress.com/view/carmillatheopera.wordpress.com

The full text of the novella is available at Project Gutenberg: http://www.gutenberg.org/ebooks/10007

La Mama Theatre: http://lamama.com.au/

www.ingramcontent.com/pod-product-compliance
Lightning Source LLC
Chambersburg PA
CBHW050028090426
42734CB00021B/3464